ART AND NATURE:
THE GARDENS AT SUNNYLANDS

With essays by James Burnett, Mary Irish, and Michaeleen Gallagher

THE ANNENBERG FOUNDATION TRUST
AT SUNNYLANDS

Text, design, and all images copyright
© The Annenberg Foundation Trust at Sunnylands 2014.

First published in 2014 by The Annenberg Foundation Trust at Sunnylands,
PO Box 1710, Rancho Mirage, CA 92270, United States of America.

All rights reserved. No part of this book may be reproduced or utilized,
in any form or by any means, electronic or mechanical, without prior
permission in writing from the publisher.

Library of Congress Control Number: 2013957052

ISBN: 978-0-9858429-7-0. Printed in the United States of America.

Photography by Mark Davidson.
Additional photographs provided by Sibylle Allgaier, Dillon Diers,
Michaeleen Gallagher, Daniel Modlin, Mary Perry, and Danielle Sombati.

Book and cover design by JCRR Design.

The Annenberg Retreat at Sunnylands by Geoffrey Cowan	page 6
Sunnylands Center & Gardens by Janice Lyle, Ph.D.	page 6
Gardens Vision by James Burnett	pages 8 – 11
The Collection by Mary Irish	pages 12 – 19
The Gardens Realized by Michaeleen Gallagher	pages 20 – 23
Plants Portfolio	pages 24 – 167
Acknowledgments	page 168

Symbols in the plants portfolio section provide the reader with pertinent information about each featured plant.

Maximum size

Bloom color

Bloom season

Wildlife benefit

Human benefit

Awareness

Fold out the front flap of this book to reference these symbols while reading.

The Annenberg Retreat at Sunnylands

For more than forty years, Sunnylands served as an oasis for presidents of the United States, other heads of state, and leaders from government, business, education, science, and the arts—a place for reflection, relaxation, and conversation.

Believing that the beauty of the setting could inspire a unique brand of informal, collegial, and productive deliberations, Walter and Leonore Annenberg created The Annenberg Retreat at Sunnylands as a venue for small, high-level meetings designed to advance world peace, facilitate international agreements, and create solutions to important problems. They also wanted the public to have access to Sunnylands to experience its beauty, art, and history.

The Trustees developed Sunnylands Center & Gardens as the public access point where visitors can learn about the history of the Annenbergs and the important guests whom they entertained at Sunnylands. The continuing work of the Trust, the significance of the Midcentury Modern architecture, the art collection, and Hollywood Regency furnishings add to the uniqueness of this special place.

The arid-landscape plants in this garden provide an amazing array of experiences for the general public. I am so pleased that this publication will introduce the beauty of the Gardens to those who haven't yet visited and offer ongoing memories for those who have savored its sights, smells, and sounds.

Geoffrey Cowan
President, The Annenberg Foundation Trust at Sunnylands

Sunnylands Center & Gardens

This book highlights the vision of Sunnylands Gardens as outlined by the landscape designer, the plant choices made by the horticulturist, and the current public uses of the space as programmed by Sunnylands staff.

The impact of the Gardens on the public has exceeded any of our expectations. It has matured quickly and its constantly changing bloom cycle means that each month the experience is subtly and/or dramatically different.

The visual impact is immediate and visceral for our guests. It is unlike any other desert garden they have seen and therefore it encourages them to think differently about the essential qualities of desert plants. This emphasis on the aesthetics of the Gardens also sets our project apart from others.

We proudly proclaim that this is an art garden, not a botanic garden. We have interesting plant specimens but the core sensibility features the colors, shapes, and textures that are created by the massing of single species. Placing areas of mass plantings next to each other highlights the brushstroke-like quality of this landscape and connects it to the Impressionist and Post-Impressionist painting collection of the Annenbergs. As an introduction to the Annenberg story, the Gardens references the high level of taste and the fascination with art shared by Walter and Leonore Annenberg.

The purpose of the Center & Gardens is to introduce the public to the Annenberg legacy and to make that legacy alive and relevant. By creating the Gardens, the Trust has provided a contemporary commentary on the historic landscape—a dialogue between the 21st and 20th centuries about the ways in which natural resources are used and beauty is defined. That conversation should be lively and vibrant for many years to come.

Janice Lyle, Ph.D.
Director, Sunnylands Center & Gardens

GARDENS VISION

James Burnett *Founder/President, The Office of James Burnett*

In August 2006, I was contacted by architect Frederick Fisher about a new opportunity in Rancho Mirage for The Annenberg Foundation Trust at Sunnylands. Fisher described the project as a visitor center for the Annenberg estate. Sunnylands Center would be open to the public and would tell the story of the Annenbergs and their involvement in public policy, education, and the arts. The Center would also complement the retreat mission where high-level leaders could conduct discussions securely and privately. My firm's contribution would be to design the Gardens, which would support the mission by creating a serene setting.

The idea of teaming with Frederick Fisher and Partners on such a significant historical property and the opportunity to work with Leonore Annenberg were very exciting to me. I knew of the Annenbergs from their many philanthropic activities as well as their love of art and design. We submitted our portfolio, along with some conceptions of what the Gardens might feel like in the future. We were honored that Leonore Annenberg selected us, and in mid-November 2006 we began the design effort with our first visit to the property. Dillon Diers, our project manager who joined the firm a few weeks before we won the commission, spearheaded the site analysis.

We started the process by getting to know Rancho Mirage's setting, the Coachella Valley, as well as the history of the estate. We worked closely with the Fisher team and The Annenberg Foundation Trust at Sunnylands to determine the proportions of the 15-acre site for the Center & Gardens, which was selected in large part for its proximity to the estate. It is just across the property line on the north from the 200-acre grounds surrounding the magnificent Midcentury Modern Annenberg house, separated by an existing tamarisk hedge. Another important consideration was the visual context: the site offers a dramatic vista of the San Jacinto Mountains to the west and glimpses of the estate between the tamarisks to the south. We developed a clear understanding of the natural environment and began to prepare design concepts.

Our first meetings with Leonore Annenberg were focused on the big ideas for Sunnylands Center & Gardens. How would it relate to the landscape of the estate and golf course on the other side of the tamarisk hedge? Would the properties speak the same language, or, because they were created in different eras, should they be different? These were very important discussion points for our team, the building architects, and the client. Initially, we were looking for a way to integrate the two properties conceptually but, as we pushed deeper into the process, it was clear that the landscapes of the estate and the Center would inevitably be different. However, there would be some similarities in the features, such as the entry drive, the entry arrival court, and the garden terraces surrounding the buildings.

We wanted to create a sense of separation from the busy traffic along Bob Hope Drive and bring people to Sunnylands Center through a rich and multilayered sequence. The entry approach was designed to take visitors away from the everyday world and into a new experience, a landscape arrangement that would be both thought-provoking and moving. We also wanted to connect the Gardens with the beautifully simple and elegant building that Fisher and his team created. The garden terraces surrounding the Center, like the building itself, would be crisp and modern, adorned with single-species

Opposite James Burnett discusses his vision for the Gardens.

Below Installation required meticulous placement of specimens and irrigation lines.

trays of plantings; they would resonate with the very tailored details of the building. We intended these terraces to work well for the many events to be programmed at the Center. The garden pattern would loosen up, changing and becoming less predictable, as one moved farther away from the building.

Leonore Annenberg loved color in the landscape and was very fond of the blooms created by the yellow palo verde trees in the spring. She liked the gardens and lawns at Sunnylands to be clean and orderly. She expressed concern about the exposed gravel and windswept sand that was so prevalent in other desert gardens she'd seen; she wanted our design to avoid this aesthetic. Our response to these concerns was to propose planting the garden densely and in such a way as to contrast textures and colors. We believed that plant selection was critical to the success of the Gardens and that large sweeps of single species would allow the area to achieve the lush feel she desired. After multiple design reviews, we created a composition that achieved the painterly approach of large brushstrokes of color through swaths of desert-appropriate plantings. The exposed gravel would be limited to a few select areas. Our goal was to make a desert garden that felt luxurious without requiring the water and supplements needed for a traditional, heavily groomed garden.

As a client, Leonore Annenberg was ideal; she trusted our judgment and gave us the freedom to implement our design concepts. However, she challenged us along the way. She was very concerned about the way a visitor might experience the Gardens, from the very moment his car's front wheels rolled onto the entry drive. She was curious about the various garden paths we'd incorporated into the design and, in particular,

wanted to understand the visual connection between the Gardens and the building. We created a series of renderings to illustrate the views at each step along the entry and garden sequence, refining our own vision as we clarified it for her. Throughout, we tried to take advantage of the spectacular view of the mountains to the west.

From a program perspective, we wanted to create a garden that would be just as interesting in November as in May, so seasonal changes and bloom schedules were key factors in our planning. The landscape "rooms," such as the labyrinth, the Great Lawn, the specimen garden, the Performance Circle, the wildflower field, and the west terrace, were intended to provide variety and encourage return visits to the Center. The idea was that people would drop by on a regular basis to take a walk in the Gardens, connect with nature, attend a class, see a friend for lunch, or just unwind from the stress of everyday life. We envisioned many places to discover throughout the Gardens, hoping to inspire and enchant its explorers.

Another of our priorities was that the Gardens be educational, serving as a paradigm of sustainable landscape design. We devised a high-efficiency irrigation system, geothermal wells below the surface, and a stormwater-capture system to eliminate all runoff. Most important, we required plant species that could handle the heat, wind, and exposure of the site. The noted horticulturist Mary Irish was instrumental in helping us choose appropriate plants, ones that were tough as well as beautiful. Irish and Diers spent a tremendous amount of time procuring the flora for the project; all of the 53,000 plants were individually selected in regional nurseries.

As the project took shape, it became clear that Sunnylands Gardens would also serve as a showcase for innovations in garden design for the Sonoran Desert: the large arcs of 50 or 100 plants of a single species, the limited plant palette (70 species) for a botanic experience, the contrast of colors blooming at different times, and the sculptural forms of the plantings taken together. We contrasted sizes and shapes, such as the height of the San Pedro cactus with the bulbous form of the barrel cactus, the star shape of Parry's agave with the spikiness of *Aloe 'Blue Elf'*, the dainty starbursts of the euphorbia gopher plant with the more robust explosions of *Yucca pallida*. We designed the plantings to be legible at different scales: from afar, as bold stripes of color; and up close, as individual plants showcasing the characteristics of each species. We used ordinary native desert plantings in unusual combinations, limiting the number of species in each composition.

We envisioned Sunnylands Gardens as a place where visitors could traverse a variety of sensory settings, delighting in the diverse smells and sights of the desert. Our goal was to craft an environment that was not only beautiful but also fascinating, to offer an experience unlike other garden experiences. We worked on the project for over five years—unfortunately, Leonore Annenberg, who passed away in 2009, did not get to see its completion—before the public arrived to partake of that experience. To our immense satisfaction, and thanks largely to the outstanding education and enrichment programs offered at the Sunnylands Center, visitors in great numbers are now using and enjoying the Gardens in ways we had not even imagined.

Opposite left
The garden pattern is carefully laid out to create layers of textures and colors.

Opposite right
Staging plant specimens under the photovoltaic field for placement in the Gardens.

Left In peak of season, palo verde trees bloom with bright yellow flowers.

Photo by Ken Hayden, 2012.

THE COLLECTION

Mary Irish *Horticultural Consultant/Garden Writer*

Garden view.

As you enter Sunnylands Center, the Gardens envelop you in the extraordinary beauty and power of desert plants. Sweeping panoramas and gentle curves invite the visitor to slow down and relish the graceful sway of flowering red yucca or be enthralled by the stunning sculptures of the green-barked palo verdes.

Here, in one of the hottest and driest corners of the world, James Burnett and his associate Dillon Diers took the challenges of the climate, soils, and limited water of the Coachella Valley and worked with them to create one of the most original and exciting desert gardens anywhere. This is a garden that celebrates and embraces its desert home rather than conquers or subdues it.

It was far from an accident and it almost didn't happen. When Leonore Annenberg began the process of transforming Sunnylands—the winter home she shared with her husband Walter Annenberg—into a retreat center for world leaders and other international figures as well as a public place to celebrate their lives, a garden was envisioned as part of the public entry. It was originally conceived as a complement to the expansive park-like vistas of Sunnylands, with sweeping lawns punctuated by large trees and dimpled with lakes.

But Burnett had another idea—why not feature the desert where Sunnylands was located and use plants from deserts to create a garden as bold, creative, and lasting as the legacy of the Annenbergs themselves. He believed that the Gardens should be as important and original as Sunnylands itself. Following a series of discussions, Leonore Annenberg was convinced and a revolutionary new plan for the Gardens began to take shape.

The final design was deeply influenced by the extensive Impressionist and Post-Impressionist paintings that the Annenbergs had assembled throughout their lives. A painter himself, Burnett began to see in the mighty brush strokes, strong colors, and vivid lines of these artists, particularly Van Gogh, the style and outline of the garden for this site.

Leonore Annenberg established few criteria for the plants: yellow flowers were preferred, palms were not to be included, and the entire garden was to be lush and beautiful. Burnett and his team added that the plants must be from arid or desert regions, be able to thrive in the scalding heat, use minimal water, and be as uniform as possible.

At just over nine acres, the Gardens needed a breathtaking number of plants to secure the great lines of color and texture that Burnett envisioned. In the end, over 53,000 plants make up the Gardens. It took three years to find them all and work with the various growers to achieve the exacting specifications of the design. Many sections were laid out plant-by-plant to ensure that the curves flowed like waves of sand on a windy day and that views emerged and faded as visitors moved through the Gardens. The result is a garden where all elements—land, plants, and design—blend seamlessly, creating a living painting that reflects the genuine scope and majesty of the desert.

Trees and Shrubs

Wind is a critical concern in the Coachella Valley. Relentless and often devastating, wind speeds can reach up to 60 mph or more. At both the original estate and in the Gardens, the first line of defense in managing the wind is stopping it with dense hedges.

The need for a hedge that would slow down the wind, and its load of fine sand, was recognized from the beginning. The Indian laurel figs *(Ficus microcarpa)* and tamarisk *(Tamarisk aphylla)* used on the original estate did not match the criteria for this garden. The team decided to use the South Texas native, Texas ebony *(Ebenopsis ebano)*. This is a thorny, intricately branched shrub typically pruned to a tree, which is left here to grow virtually to the ground.

This hedge not only helps hold back the wind and sand, but forms a deep green, living boundary between the Gardens and the utility buildings, drives, parking areas, street, and natural desert. It is the backdrop of the entire Gardens. Once it was installed, the Gardens became a unit enclosed on all sides—not quite a hidden garden, but where the only outside view was the majestic rise of the San Jacinto and Santa Rosa Mountains behind the Center.

Trees at Sunnylands Center & Gardens are some of the most visible parts of the garden, particularly the 'Desert Museum' palo verdes that surround the Great Lawn. These trees, with their smooth green bark and brilliant yellow bloom, clasp the boundaries of the lawn like a bracelet forming an arch of shade as visitors stroll through the west garden. These trees are a pathway that guide visitors to the small Performance Circle, past collections of yucca, agave, golden barrels, and ocotillo, to the labyrinth, and ultimately back "home" to the Center.

Following the rectangular lines of the Center are two blocks of closely spaced palo brea *(Parkinsonia praecox)*. Native to Sonora, Mexico this tree has slick green bark and a sinuous branching habit that combine to give it the look of a dancer's pose. These trees form a canopy over the smooth agave *(Agave murpheyi)* on one end, and pale-leaf yucca *(Yucca pallida)* on the other.

Texas ebony *(Ebenopsis ebano)*

Palo Verde *(Parkinsonia x 'Desert Museum')*

Sweet acacia *(Acacia farnesiana)*

Far right *Leucophyllum frutescens* 'Green Cloud'
Near right Mesquite *(Prosopis hybrids)*

The design team felt that the entry court required a signature tree at each of its corners and the densely branched sweet acacia *(Acacia farnesiana)* was ideal. A tree of the arid grasslands of south Texas and Mexico, it is best known for its smothering bloom of intensely fragrant, golden flowers in late winter. In February and March their sweet aroma guides visitors into the Center.

Desert plants have evolved a wide and impressive array of adaptations to the intense heat, low rainfall, and nitrogen-poor soils of most deserts. One of these adaptations, small leaves that are broken into tiny fragments, is vividly displayed by the hundreds of hybrid palo verdes *(Parkinsonia hybrids)* and hybrid mesquites *(Prosopis hybrids)* throughout the Gardens.

The tiny leaves in the multi-branched palo verde provide abundant shade for visitors, plants, and wildlife and, like all palo verde, have a resplendent yellow bloom in the spring and striking green bark.

Mesquite, with its dusky green leaves, twisting limbs, and black bark, is spaced throughout the Gardens and its walkways to provide intermittent shade. These trees are most abundant in the beds surrounding the Great Lawn, along the walkway of the retention basin, and around a wildflower field. Benches throughout the Gardens are sheltered by these trees. Mesquites also provide a measure of cold protection for selected plantings in the Gardens.

Parking lots are by their nature hot, often uninviting locations. Trees to shade the parking lot needed to be tall but fairly fast growing, able to be pruned high without losing their aesthetic appeal, and of desert origin. A hybrid mesquite *(Prosopis hybrid)* that grew to such dimensions was selected. It satisfies these requirements and is also the tree around the labyrinth on the south side of the Great Lawn.

Shrubs form a backdrop to the textured or colorful plantings of the Gardens. All the shrubs are various species of Texas Ranger. *Leucophyllum langmaniae* and its selection 'Lynn's Legacy' is easily recognized by its small, dark green foliage and deeply congested purple flowers. The hybrid 'Heavenly Cloud' has similar foliage but blue flowers. *Leucophyllum frutescens* 'Green Cloud' is the largest of the group with dark green leaves and deep magenta flowers, while fragrant sage *(L. pruinosum)* has pale gray leaves and pink-purple flowers. Chihuahuan sage *(L. laevigatum)* has a spreading habit, deep green leaves, and dark purple flowers. These evergreen shrubs are planted along the boundary of a wildflower field, beneath the parking lot mesquites, and throughout the retention basin. These shrubs are easily taken for granted until suddenly in the late summer the entire plant is transformed into a dark purple, deep mauve, pink, or lavender hedge.

Perennials

One of the greatest challenges for the design team was finding perennials that met the twin needs of the conditions of the site and yellow bloom. The most prominent perennial planting is the border between the flat expanse of the Great Lawn and the tall palo verdes. Here the low-growing, deep green of green santolina *(Santolina rosmarinifolia)* seemed ideal, but this species proved difficult to maintain the strict uniformity required by the design. Damianita *(Chrysactinia mexicana)* is now installed and has shown itself to be a star performer. This rugged evergreen perennial has brilliant yellow flowers in the spring that smother the tidy plant and mirror the bright palo verde bloom.

Far right Damianita *(Chrysactinia mexicana)*
Near right *Leucophyllum x* 'Heavenly Cloud'

Desert milkweed *(Asclepias subulata)*

Gopher plant *(Euphorbia rigida)*

Medicinal aloe *(Aloe vera)*

Coral aloe *(Aloe striata)*

Another prominent and immensely successful perennial is the desert milkweed *(Asclepias subulata)*. Planted in great drifts, these wispy stemmed plants send up abundant masses of creamy flower heads in the spring. They are a favored food plant for a number of butterflies and their larvae, and are the anchor of numerous areas of the west garden and the front entry gardens.

Along the drive look for trailing smokebush *(Dalea greggii)* with its dusky green-to-gray leaves. This is also the plant that forms the labyrinth. Other prominent perennials include gopher plant *(Euphorbia rigida)*, with its striking chartreuse bracts (modified leaves that mimic flowers) through the spring, and Angelita daisy *(Tetraneuris acaulis)*, a deep green mound of a plant with tall, yellow, daisy-like flowers. These species are found mainly along the entry drive and form a visual interruption between the hard edges of the succulents and the pavement.

The Succulents

To many people, succulents—cacti in particular—are the essence of a desert plant. These remarkable plants are found in a wide variety of plant families, in both the New and the Old Worlds. They all share a common feature. They have specialized tissues that retain water that can be used for the critical work of photosynthesis when soil moisture is depleted. In cactus these cells are in the stems; in aloes these cells are in the leaves.

In the Gardens, aloes are the most commonly used succulent. The striking aloe hybrid 'Blue Elf' punctuates the plantings along the drive with its blue-gray, linear leaves standing upright against the fierce desert sun. The crowded heads of deep coral flowers in the late winter and early spring just add to its appeal.

The well-known medicinal aloe *(Aloe vera)*, which has been cultivated for centuries for its ability to soothe minor abrasions and burns, forms significant displays throughout the Gardens but particularly around the Performance Circle and behind the Great Lawn. It fills the beds completely with its tall, upright stately leaves. The forest of yellow or orange flowering spikes draws in hummingbirds and other nectar-feeding wildlife.

Coral aloe *(Aloe striata)* has wide, blue-gray leaves rimmed in pink and accents beds behind the Great Lawn. Like most aloes, this species prefers the dappled shade of the mesquites and palo verdes to thrive.

Cardon (Pachycereus pringlei)

Blue barrel (Ferocactus glaucescens)

Golden barrel (Echinocactus grusonii)

Red barrel (Ferocactus pilosus)

Smooth agave (Agave desmettiana)

Cacti

Cacti in the Gardens are restricted to the Specimen Garden on the north side of the Center and the golden barrel cactus plantings.

In the Specimen Garden, a selection of striking cactus include wooly torch *(Espostoa melenostele)*, organ pipe *(Stenocereus thurberi)*, Mexican fence post *(Pachycereus marginatus)*, and cardon *(Pachycereus pringlei)* that all stand as tall sentinels. Smaller cactus like blue barrel *(Ferocactus glaucescens)* and red barrel *(Ferocactus pilosus)*, as well as succulents like Medusa head *(Euphorbia caput-medusae)* and red aloe *(Aloe ferox)*, fill in the bed.

Golden barrel cactus *(Echinocactus grusonii)* is one of the cactus world's stars with its rigid, rounded form and brilliant yellow spines. Look for it under the shade of the palo breas near the Center and in a remarkable planting to the south of the Great Lawn. Here the ground is covered with black scoria and the tall San Pedro cactus *(Echinopsis pachanoi)* and golden barrel cactus are set like twin jewels on the dark base. This dramatic presentation is one of the artistic gems visitors find while wandering through the Gardens.

The Agaves and Yuccas

Early in the design process, Burnett and his team saw the potential that the tight rosette forms of agaves and yuccas could bring to the design. Coupled with the ease with which they live in the desert, these plants were a natural choice and are found throughout the Gardens.

The generous plantings of smooth agave *(Agave desmettiana)* around the Center and along the entry drive show off some of the best features of agaves. This species grows as a small fountain of deep green, almost glossy leaves. The color, size, and shape plus the remarkable uniformity within the group appealed immediately to the design team. These plants line the front of the building, wrap around its southern and western sides, and provide a vivid base that enhances the clean lines of the Center.

Flowering of these agaves began as early as 2013 and the sturdy stalks of deep golden flowers are a show all their own. In this species, small plants known as bulbils form after flowering. Some are collected to grow out for replacements so that the continuity of the design is assured.

Desert agave *(Agave deserti)* is a local native planted abundantly throughout the Gardens. The blue-green somewhat linear leaves are particularly effective in the retention basin and along the gardens on the west side of the Center. From the vista of the walkway that surrounds the retention basin, these plants form the strong bands of color that Burnett sought.

Artichoke agave *(Agave parryi var. truncata)* is easily recognized by its rounded blue-green leaves lined with maroon edges, teeth, and terminal spines. These are tidy plants that form a nearly perfect globe when well grown. Used generously, as they are here, they create a stunning pattern. The smaller black-spined agave *(Agave macroacantha)*, found near the labyrinth, have narrow smoky blue-gray leaves with the maroon margins, teeth, and terminal spine. Agaves of great size, century plant *(Agave americana)* and green giant agave *(Agave salmiana)*, were used in the back corners of the Gardens where their spread could be accommodated.

On the back side of the Great Lawn is a small planting of the most unusual agave in the Gardens—*Agave titanota*. Here uniformity had to give way to the free-form growth habit of this species, a trait well regarded by collectors. The variety of leaf size and color, size and shape of teeth and spines, and overall size and habit of the plant are astounding. These features and its scarcity dictated that it be given a small bed of its own so that the visitor could stop a minute and look closely at each and every individual.

Yuccas are in the same family as agaves, but contribute an entirely different look to the Gardens. Yucca flowers, like agave, are on stalks high above the foliage but are pure white. Unlike agave, however, the plant does not die after flowering.

Pale-leaf yucca *(Yucca pallida)* forms the floor beneath the palo breas on the north. This small yucca from west central Texas has deep-blue to dusky blue-gray leaves, often with prominent veins. Plants have relatively few leaves and, when planted closely as they are here, look like a smoky film over the ground.

Beaked yucca (Yucca rostrata)

Beaked yucca *(Yucca rostrata)* is used sparingly in the Gardens, chiefly as a punctuation behind the wildflower field. This tall, tree-like yucca will become a focal point at the back of the field as it matures. The heads are packed with hundreds of thin leaves that have a ribbon of pale yellow along the edge, which becomes prominent when plants are backlit, making them appear to erupt into flame.

Other Desert Plants

Plants rarely fit into neat and tidy categories: succulent, perennial, shrub, and so forth. No group defies these categories with more vigor than nolinas, hesperaloe, and ocotillo.

Nolinas look much like a grass, which they are not; are as tough and rugged as yucca, which they are not; yet in any hot, arid area these plants are among the finest choices for their blend of delicate texture and endurance for arid conditions. In this garden, Lindheimer's beargrass *(Nolina lindheimeriana)* was chosen for its rounded, soft lines similar to a bunch grass but without the water requirements. The firm, thin green leaves never need to be sheared or pruned back. It is one of the anchors of the retention basin as it weaves its way through the design.

Red hesperaloe (Hesperaloe parviflora)

Red hesperaloe *(Hesperaloe parviflora)* with its tightly held, dusky green leaves is widely planted around a wildflower field, along the entry drive, within the retention basin, and in small areas

17

Ocotillo *(Fouquieria splendens)*

Desert primrose *(Oenothera deltoidea)*

California poppy *(Eschscholtzia californica)*

Multi-species in the Wildflower Field

behind the Great Lawn. In the spring, tall spires of coral-to-pink flowers nod and fall creating one of the most intense visual displays in the Gardens. The flowers are immensely attractive to hummingbirds, moths, and a wide array of insects.

Behind the Performance Circle is the large hybrid between the giant hesperaloe *(Hesperaloe funifera)* and the red hesperaloe. This is a tall plant with upright leaves that sends up huge stalks filled with coral flowers later in the spring. It helps carry the color through the Gardens into the early summer.

Small forests of ocotillo *(Fouquieria splendens)* are scattered throughout the Gardens—at the east end of the retention basin and in the small beds behind the Great Lawn, in particular. Ocotillo grows numerous tall, spiny canes that have deep green but intermittent leaves. Long spires of bright red flowers at the tips bloom throughout the year and are a favorite of hummingbirds for both their nectar and as a perch.

Wildlflower Field

The wildflower field, like the retention basin, also serves as a rainfall retention area. It was hydroseeded with a blend of native grasses, annuals, and perennials. Prominent species include desert primrose *(Oenothera deltoidea)* with big, white flowers; sand verbena *(Abronia villosa)* with a sprawling habit and deep purple flowers; the tall, yellow-flowering brittlebush *(Encelia farinose)*; and the intense golden flowers of California poppy *(Eschscholtzia californica)*. Anchored by native grasses such as purple threeawn *(Aristida purpurea)*, this is one of the best places in the Gardens to find native lizards, insects, and seed-eating birds.

Gardens never sit still; they are shifting and changing as soon as the first plant goes in. But great ones have a design that endures such change and are formed of plants that are well-suited to the location. Such gardens are enhanced and renewed, rather than diminished, by the twists and turns of time.

The Gardens at Sunnylands Center is one of the finest examples of these two principles in action—spectacular any day you see them, never quite the same from season to season, year to year, but always firm in its celebration of the plants of the deserts. The garden is both restful and stimulating, lively and calm, and always resounds with the artistry and vision of its designer.

Background trees (*parkinsonia* 'Desert Museum'), mid-ground red planting (*hesperaloe parviflora*), and foreground planting (*leucophyllum langmoniae*)

THE GARDENS REALIZED

Michaeleen Gallagher *Director of Education and Environmental Programs*

Above Quiet trails encourage exploration.

Right Music students collaborate with symphony musicians.

Sunnylands Center & Gardens engages visitors on an interactive level. Public programming and partnerships have created a community space where visitors return again and again. Desert plants become part of exhibitions as art displayed in the glass-walled exhibition gallery is backed by succulents planted just outside the glass. Themed programs place sculptors and painters within the Gardens interacting with visitors. Architectural partnerships offer programming with a "then and now" historical and contemporary perspective of building design and use. Natural history and hands-on environmental education allow exploration of topics including horticulture, the ecology of native pollinators, and arid-landscape design. This public engagement adds a final layer to the Gardens, a sense of connection with the community to which the Center & Gardens is a gift.

The Gardens opened to the public in March 2012 to reveal a visually spectacular nine acres of arid-landscape planting. Leonore Annenberg initiated the project in 2006 and worked closely with James Burnett, the landscape architect who designed the Gardens. After her death in 2009, the Annenberg Foundation Trust at Sunnylands continued the project to its completion.

James Burnett brought years of experience creating spaces designed for quiet reflection to the project. Calming elements have been included in every part of the Gardens. On the perimeter, trees and hedges buffer the sounds of city traffic and block strong desert winds. Within the Gardens, a labyrinth has been included to encourage meditative walking. Footsteps on decomposed granite paths, activities of wildlife, and two water features create a space of focused natural sounds.

When completed, over 53,000 plant specimens had been carefully laid out in a design inspired by the Impressionist artwork of Vincent Van Gogh. Texture,

color, and light were carefully considered in plant selection and placement.

The Center & Gardens communicate a connection to the historic estate. The entry drive, which presents a "hide and reveal" effect for visitors as they approach the Center, follows the same design as the drive leading to the historic house. Berms and retention basins simulate the rise and fall of the greens and fairways of the golf course. Although architectural design and layout reference the estate, the Gardens maintains its own uniqueness in scope and visual effect. This constructed landscape encourages dialogues on the changing views of the environment.

Plant selection included only arid-adapted species. Succulents, desert shrubs, and native trees selected in a range of greens, blues, and grays are planted in single-specimen massings, designed to create layers of color and texture that provide year-round visual interest. Vistas throughout the Gardens provide unexpected views, including a breathtaking panorama of Mount San Jacinto. There are also smaller gardenscapes revealed along winding paths and an annual blooming wildflower field.

Above Students participate in citizen science programs.

Below Third Sundays offer educational programs and activities for all ages.

Left Films on the Great Lawn highlight one of many community partnerships.

Below A lion dancer engages children as part of a cultural celebration.

Beginning in late winter and continuing through early summer, changing color palettes in the desert bloom cycle add a new visual layer. Beginning with the yellows and reds of the winter-blooming aloes, such as aloe vera, blue elf, and striata, and ending with the pinks and whites of the late-blooming hesperaloes and nolinas, the Gardens offers a new experience on each visit. In April, when the bloom cycle reaches its peak, palo verdes and palo brea trees move the line of sight from plants along the ground to the sky by presenting canopies of bright yellow blooms attracting both wildlife and the largest seasonal crowds.

Visitors entering the Gardens glimpse their first view of the world of Walter and Leonore Annenberg. The historic estate preserves the Annenberg legacy, and through its education and environmental programs, the Center & Gardens interprets the Annenberg story for the public.

Left The plein air series provides exclusive access for artists.

Opposite A health and wellness program includes free yoga classes.

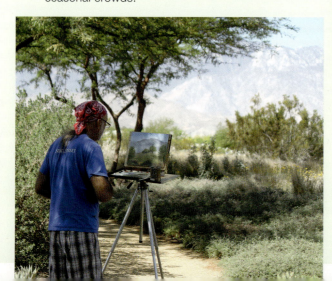

Sweet Acacia
Acacia farnesiana

- 15-25 feet high
- yellow-orange
- winter, spring
- bees, birds, small mammals
- aromatic, perfume, ornamental, shade
- thorns, some toxic compounds

TREE

Texas Ebony
Ebenopsis ebano

- 25-30 feet high
- white, fuzzy spike
- summer
- bees, birds, butterflies, small mammals
- aromatic, ornamental
- thorns

Desert Museum Palo Verde

Parkinsonia x 'Desert Museum'

- 25 feet high
- bright yellow
- spring, summer
- bees, birds, butterflies, small mammals
- ornamental, shade
- N/A

TREE

Palo Brea
Parkinsonia praecox

- 20-30 feet high
- bright yellow
- early spring, summer
- bees, birds, butterflies, small mammals
- ornamental, shade
- thorns

Mesquite
Prosopis multi-species and hybrids

- 20-40 feet high
- yellow
- summer
- bees, birds, butterflies, small mammals
- ornamental, thornless, shade, food
- N/A

Century Plant
Agave americana

- 6 feet high × 13 wide
- cream
- infrequent
- birds, bats
- ornamental
- some toxic compounds, sharp foliage

AGAVE

Variegated Caribbean Agave

Agave angustifolia variegata

- 3 feet high × 8 wide
- green to yellow
- infrequent
- birds, bats, insects
- fiber, food
- some toxic compounds, sharp foliage

AGAVE

Blue Flame Agave

Agave x 'Blue Flame'

- 2 feet high x 4 wide
- yellow-green
- infrequent
- birds, bats, insects
- ornamental
- some toxic compounds, sharp foliage

Cow's Horn Agave
Agave bovicornuta

- 2-3 feet high x 3-5 wide
- yellow-green
- infrequent
- birds, bats, insects
- ornamental
- some toxic compounds, sharp foliage

Desert Agave
Agave deserti

- 19 inches high × 24 wide
- bright yellow
- infrequent
- birds, insects, mammals
- ornamental, food
- some toxic compounds, sharp foliage

Smooth Agave
Agave desmettiana

- 3 feet high
- pale yellow
- infrequent
- birds, insects, small mammals
- ornamental
- some toxic compounds, sharp foliage

AGAVE

Twin-Flowered Agave
Agave geminiflora

- 2-3 feet high and wide
- greenish yellow-tinged red
- infrequent
- birds, insects, mammals
- ornamental
- some toxic compounds, sharp foliage

AGAVE

Thorn-Crested Agave

Agave lophantha 'Quadricolor'

- 1 foot high × 2 wide
- pale yellow
- infrequent
- bees, butterflies, mammals
- ornamental
- some toxic compounds, sharp foliage

Black-Spined Agave
Agave macroacantha

- 16 inches high and wide
- green-tinged purple
- infrequent
- bats, insects, mammals
- ornamental
- some toxic compounds, sharp foliage

AGAVE

Murphey's Agave
Agave murpheyi

- 3-4 feet high and 4-5 wide
- yellow
- infrequent
- birds, bats, insects
- ornamental
- some toxic compounds, sharp foliage

Parry's Agave
Agave parryi

- 2 feet high × 3 wide
- yellow
- infrequent
- birds, insects, mammals
- ornamental, food
- some toxic compounds, sharp foliage

Artichoke Agave
Agave parryi
var. truncata

- 2 feet high × 3 wide
- golden yellow
- infrequent
- birds, insects, mammals
- ornamental
- some toxic compounds, sharp foliage

AGAVE

Sharkskin Agave
Agave 'Sharkskin'

- 2-3 feet high × 3-4 wide
- green
- infrequent
- bats, insects
- ornamental
- some toxic compounds, sharp foliage

AGAVE

Agave titanota

- 30 inches wide
- yellow tinged lavender
- infrequent
- birds, insects, mammals
- ornamental
- some toxic compounds, sharp foliage

AGAVE

Blue Elf Aloe
Aloe 'Blue Elf' hybrid

- 3 feet high x 2 wide
- orange-red
- winter, spring
- birds, insects, small mammals
- ornamental
- some toxic compounds

Coral Aloe
Aloe striata

- 2 feet high × 2 wide
- red-orange
- winter, spring
- birds, insects
- ornamental
- some toxic compounds

Medicinal Aloe
Aloe vera

- 2 feet high × 2 wide
- yellow and orange
- winter, spring
- birds
- ornamental, medicinal
- N/A

Giant Hesperaloe
Hesperaloe funifera

- 4 feet high × 4 wide
- creamy-white with pink-green blush
- spring, summer, fall
- birds
- ornamental, fiber
- sharp foliage

Funifera Hybrid Hesperaloe

Hesperaloe funifera × H. parviflora

- 6 feet high × 6 wide
- pink
- summer, fall
- birds
- ornamental
- some toxic compounds, sharp foliage

Red Hesperaloe
Hesperaloe parviflora

- 3 feet high × 4 wide
- red to pink
- spring, summer
- birds
- ornamental, paper fibers
- sharp foliage

Brake-lights Red Yucca

Hesperaloe parviflora 'Perpa' P.P.A.F. Brakelights

- 2 feet high
- bright red
- spring, summer, fall
- hummingbirds
- ornamental
- sharp foliage

HESPERALOE

Pale-leaf Yucca
Yucca pallida

- 1 foot high × 2 wide
- white
- summer
- moths, giant skipper butterfly larval host
- ornamental
- sharp foliage

Beaked Yucca
Yucca rostrata

- 4–7 feet high
- white
- summer
- moths, bats
- ornamental
- sharp foliage

YUCCA

Our Lord's Candle
Yucca whipplei

- 3 feet high × 4 wide
- white
- infrequent
- moths, bats
- ornamental
- sharp foliage

ART AND NATURE: THE GARDENS AT SUNNYLANDS

82

Madagascar Ocotillo
Alluaudia procera

- 30 feet high
- orange, gold, pale yellow
- late spring, summer
- insects, birds, mammals
- ornamental
- some toxic compounds, sharp foliage

DIDIEREA

ART AND NATURE: THE GARDENS AT SUNNYLANDS

Desert Milkweed
Asclepias subulata

- 4 feet high × 2 wide
- creamy-yellow
- spring, summer, fall
- pollinator insect species
- ornamental, attracts pollinators
- some toxic compounds

Damianita
Chrysactinia mexicana

- 12 inches high × 24 wide
- bright yellow
- spring, summer, fall
- birds, insects
- fragrant ornamental, rabbit resistant
- N/A

ASTER

Angelita Daisy
Tetraneuris acaulis

- 12 inches high x 18 wide
- yellow
- spring, summer, fall
- bees
- ornamental
- N/A

Desert Marigold
Baileya multiradiata

- 18 inches high x 24 wide
- bright yellow
- spring, summer, fall
- insects
- ornamental, long blooming
- N/A

ASTER

Brittlebush
Encelia farinosa

- 3 feet high × 3 wide
- yellow
- spring, early summer
- birds, bees, butterflies, small mammals
- ornamental
- N/A

ASTER

Trailing Smokebush
Dalea greggii

- 1 foot high × 4 wide
- purple
- spring, summer
- bees, larval host of several butterfly species
- ornamental
- N/A

Ocotillo
Fouqueria splendens

- 20 feet high × 15 wide
- red
- spring
- birds, insects, small mammals
- ornamental
- thorny trunk

Buckhorn Cholla
Cylindropuntia acanthocarpa

- 5 feet
- yellow to red
- summer
- insects, small mammals, birds
- medicinal, ornamental
- some toxic compounds, spines

Night-blooming Cactus

Cereus hildemannianus 'monstrosa'

- 15 feet high
- white
- spring, fall
- mammals, insects, birds
- food source, ornamental
- sharp foliage

Silver Torch
Cleistocactus strausii

- 10 feet high
- dark red
- winter, spring
- birds
- ornamental
- some toxic compounds, sharp spines

CACTUS

Golden Barrel
Echinocactus grusonii

- 3-4 feet high × 3 wide
- yellow
- spring, summer
- bees
- ornamental
- some toxic compounds, sharp spines

San Pedro
Echinopsis pachanoi

- 6-10 feet high
- white, night-blooming
- midsummer
- bats, moths
- ornamental
- some toxic compounds

Wooly Torch
Espostoa melanostele

- 6-7 feet high
- brown with a slight blush, hairy scales
- spring, summer
- bats, moths
- ornamental
- some toxic compounds

CACTUS

Blue Barrel
Ferocactus glaucescens

- 18 inches high × 20 wide
- yellow
- spring
- bees, butterflies
- ornamental
- some toxic compounds, spines

CACTUS

Red Barrel
Ferocactus pilosus

- 12 inches high × 20 wide
- yellow to red
- spring
- insects, small mammals
- ornamental
- some toxic compounds, spines

Bunny Ears Prickly Pear
Opuntia microdasys

- 3 feet high
- yellow-reddish tint
- spring, summer
- birds, insects, small mammals
- ornamental, food
- sharp, glochid-type spines

CACTUS

Mexican Fence Post
Pachycereus marginatus

- 16 feet high
- red
- spring, summer
- birds, insects
- boundary fence, ornamental
- some toxic compounds, spines

CACTUS

Cardón
Pachycereus pringlei

- 50 feet high
- white
- late spring, summer
- birds, insects
- ornamental, medicinal, containers
- some toxic compounds, spines

CACTUS

Blue Columnar Cactus

Pilosocereus pachycladus

- 13 feet high
- white
- summer
- bats, birds, insects
- ornamental
- sharp foliage

Organ Pipe Cactus
Stenocereus thurberi

- 26 feet high
- white, night-blooming
- summer
- bats, moths
- ornamental, food, medicine
- some toxic compounds, spines

CACTUS

Candelilla
Euphorbia antisyphillitica

- 3 feet high × 4 wide
- pinkish to cream
- late winter
- birds, insects
- ornamental, wax
- some toxic compounds

EUPHORBIA

Medusa Head
Euphorbia caput-medusae

- 39 inches high
- yellow
- spring, summer, fall
- insects
- ornamental
- some toxic compounds

EUPHORBIA

Moroccan Mound
Euphorbia resinifera

- 1-2 feet high × 6 wide
- yellow
- spring, summer
- bees
- ornamental, cosmetic industry, medicine
- some toxic compounds

Gopher Plant
Euphorbia rigida

- 2 feet high × 3 wide
- yellow
- late winter, spring
- insects
- ornamental
- some toxic compounds

African Milk Tree
euphorbia trigona

- 8 feet high × 3 wide
- white
- n/a
- n/a
- ornamental
- some toxic compounds

EUPHORBIA

Lady's Slipper

Pedilanthus macrocarpus

- 3-5 feet high × 3-5 wide
- red-orange
- fall, spring
- birds
- ornamental
- some toxic compounds

EUPHORBIA

Mexican Grass Tree

Dasylirion quadrangulatum

- 10 feet high
- cream
- late spring, summer
- birds, butterflies
- ornamental
- sharp foliage

NOLINA

Lindheimer's Beargrass
Nolina lindheimeriana

- 3-12 feet high × 4-5 wide
- white to mauve
- spring, summer
- birds, insects
- ornamental
- sharp foliage

NOLINA

Blue Nolina
Nolina nelsoni

- 3-12 feet high
- cream
- summer
- birds, insects
- ornamental
- N/A

NOLINA

Texas Ranger 'Green Cloud'

Leucophyllum frutescens x 'Green Cloud'

- 8 feet high × 8 wide
- rose-purple
- summer, fall, moisture triggered
- butterflies, bees, birds, small mammals
- ornamental
- N/A

Texas Ranger 'Heavenly Cloud'

Leucophyllum x 'Heavenly Cloud'

- 8 feet high × 6 wide
- lavender-purple
- summer, fall, moisture triggered
- butterflies, bees, birds, small mammals
- ornamental
- N/A

Chihuahuan Sage
Leucophyllum laevigatum

- 5 feet high × 3 wide
- violet
- summer, fall, moisture triggered
- butterflies, bees, birds, small mammals
- ornamental
- N/A

Texas Ranger
'Lynn's Legacy'

Leucophyllum langmaniae

- 5 feet high × 5 wide
- lavender
- summer, fall, moisture triggered
- butterflies, bees, birds, small mammals
- ornamental
- N/A

LEUCOPHYLLUM

Texas Ranger
Leucophyllum langmaniae

- 5 feet high × 3 wide
- lavender to purple
- summer, fall, moisture triggered
- butterflies, bees, birds, small mammals
- ornamental
- N/A

Sand Verbena
Abronia villosa

- 6 inches high × 20 wide
- lavender-purple
- spring, summer
- bees, butterflies
- fragrant ornamental
- N/A

ABRONIA

Purple Threeawn
Aristida purpurea

- 12-20 inches high and wide
- purple
- spring, summer, fall
- birds, butterflies
- ornamental, erosion control, root matrix
- N/A

ART AND NATURE: THE GARDENS AT SUNNYLANDS

156

Blue Grama
Bouteloua gracilis

- 14 inches
- cream to yellow
- midsummer, fall
- birds, butterflies, grazing mammals
- ornamental, accent plant, turf use
- N/A

GRASS

California Poppy
Eschscholzia californica

- 2 feet high
- orange, yellow
- late winter, spring, summer, fall
- bees, butterflies
- ornamental
- some toxic compounds

Creosote Bush
Larrea tridentata

- 5 feet high x 10 wide
- yellow
- spring, summer, fall
- birds, insects, small mammals
- medicinal, ornamental, fragrant, deer resistant
- N/A

ZYGOPHYLLUM

Dune Primrose
Oenothera deltoidea

- 10 inches high × 24 wide
- white to pinkish
- early spring
- bats, moths
- ornamental
- N/A

PRIMROSE

Desert Canterbury Bell
Phacelia campanularia

- 20 inches high × 6 wide
- blue
- spring, summer
- insect, birds
- ornamental
- skin irritant

BORAGE

Chia
Salvia columbariae

- 20 inches high
- blue
- spring, summer
- butterflies, bees
- ornamental, food
- N/A

SAGE

Acknowledgments

The Board of Trustees of The Annenberg Foundation Trust at Sunnylands provided generous support for this project. Trustees are Wallis Annenberg, Lauren Bon, Diane Deshong, Howard Deshong III, Leonore Deshong, Elizabeth R. Kabler, Liz Sorensen, Charles Annenberg Weingarten, and Gregory Annenberg Weingarten. Also supporting the Gardens and related programming was Geoffrey Cowan, President of The Annenberg Foundation Trust at Sunnylands, who conceptualized this series of Sunnylands Collections publications. Editorial oversight and direction was provided by Center Director, Janice Lyle, Ph.D.; Mary Perry, Deputy Director of Communications & Public Affairs; and Carla Breer Howard, copy editor.

The creation of the Gardens was the result of a collaborative effort among many professionals. The curatorial committee at Sunnylands included Janice Lyle, Ph.D., Center Director; Anne Rowe, Director of Collections and Exhibitions; Kathy Carr, Tour Manager & Programs Coordinator; Michaeleen Gallagher, Director of Education & Environmental Programs; and Mary Perry, Deputy Director of Communications & Public Affairs. The education and environmental programs department's efforts included those of Danielle Sombati, Education Programs Coordinator and Kelly Reynolds, Environmental Projects Coordinator. Engaged in the collections and exhibitions department's work were Daniel Modlin, Photo Archivist; Frank Lopez, Librarian and Archivist; and Kacey Donner, Collections Research Assistant. Other contributors to the project were Howard Litwak, consultant to the Trust, Patrick Truchan, Director of Operations; and Drew Kerr, Superintendent.

The Houston-based firm of The Office of James Burnett designed the Gardens. Their contributing staff included James Burnett, President; Dillon Diers, Vice President; and Mary Irish, Horticultural Consultant. Mark Davidson of Mark Davidson Photography made visually arresting images of the Gardens. Other photographs were contributed by Sibylle Allgaier, Dillon Diers, Michaeleen Gallagher, Daniel Modlin, Mary Perry, and Danielle Sombati. John Crummay and Robin Rout of JCRR Design designed this catalog and other collateral materials.